Helps to Intercession

Helps to Intercession

By Andrew Murray

CHRISTIAN LITERATURE CRUSADE
Fort Washington, Pennsylvania 19034

CHRISTIAN LITERATURE CRUSADE

U.S.A.
Box 1449, Fort Washington, PA 19034

This edition 1970

ISBN 0-87508-377-3

HELPS TO INTERCESSION

PRAY WITHOUT CEASING

Pray Without Ceasing. — Who can do this? How can one do it who is surrounded by the cares of daily life? How can a mother love her child without ceasing? How can the eyelid without ceasing hold itself ready to protect the eye? How can I breathe and feel and hear without ceasing? Because all these are the functions of a healthy, natural life. And so, if the spiritual life be healthy, under the full power of the Holy Spirit, praying without ceasing will be natural.

Pray Without Ceasing. — Does it refer to continual acts of prayer, in which we are to persevere till we obtain, or to the spirit of prayerfulness that should animate us all the day? It includes both. The example of our Lord Jesus shows us this. We have to enter our closet for special seasons of prayer; we are at times to persevere there in importunate prayer. We are also all the day to walk in God's presence, with the whole heart set upon heavenly things. Without set times of prayer, the spirit of prayer will be dull and feeble. Without the continual prayerfulness, the set times will not avail.

Pray Without Ceasing. — Does that refer to prayer for ourselves or others? To both. It is because many confine it to themselves that they fail so in practicing it. It is only when the branch gives itself to bear fruit, more fruit, much fruit, that it can live a healthy life, and expect a rich inflow of sap. The death of Christ brought Him to the place of everlasting intercession. Your death with Him to sin and self sets you free from the care of self, and elevates you to the dignity of intercessor — one who can get life and blessing from God for others. Know your calling; begin this your work. Give yourself wholly to it, and before you know it you will be finding something of this *"Praying always"* within you.

Pray Without Ceasing. — How can I learn it? The best way of learning to do a thing — in fact the only way — is *to do it*. Begin by setting apart some time every day, say ten or fifteen minutes, in which you say to God and to yourself, that you come to Him now as an intercessor for others. Let it be after your morning or evening prayer, or any other time. If you cannot secure the same time every day, do not be troubled. Only see that you do your work. Christ chose you and appointed you to pray for others.

If at first you do not feel any special urgency or faith or power in your prayers, do not let that hinder you. Quietly tell your Lord Jesus of your feebleness; believe that the Holy Spirit is in you to teach you to pray, and be assured that if you begin, God will help you. God cannot help you unless you begin and keep on.

Pray Without Ceasing. — How do I know what to pray for? If once you begin, and think of all the needs around you, you will soon find enough. But to help you, this little book is issued with subjects and hints for prayer for a month. It is meant that we should use it month by month, until we know more fully how to follow the Spirit's leading, and have learned, if need be, to make our own list of subjects, and then can dispense with it. In regard to the use of these helps, a few words may be needed.

1. *How to Pray.* — You notice for every day two headings — the one *What to Pray;* the other, *How to Pray*. If the subjects only were given, one might fall into the routine of mentioning names and things before God, and the work would become a burden. The hints under the heading *How to Pray* are meant to remind you of the spiritual nature of the work, of the need of Divine help, and to encourage faith in the certainty that God, through the Spirit, will give us grace to pray aright and will also hear our prayer. One does not at once learn to take his place boldly, and to dare to believe that he will be heard. Therefore take a few moments each day to listen to God's voice reminding you of how certainly even you will be heard, and calling on you to pray in that faith in your Father, to claim and take

the blessing you plead for. And let these words about *How to Pray* enter your hearts and occupy your thoughts at other times, too. The work of intercession is Christ's great work on earth, entrusted to Him because He gave Himself a sacrifice to God for men. The work of intercession is the greatest work a Christian can do. Give yourself as a sacrifice to God for men, and the work will become your glory and your joy, too.

2. *What to Pray.* — Scripture calls us to pray for many things: for all saints; for all men; for kings and all rulers; for all who are in adversity; for the sending forth of laborers; for those who labor in the gospel; for all converts; for believers who have fallen into sin; for one another in our own immediate circles. The Church is now so much larger than when the New Testament was written; the number of forms of work and workers is so much greater; the needs of the Church and the world are so much better known, that we need to take time and thought to see where prayer is needed, and to what our hearts are most drawn out. The Scriptural calls to prayer demand a large heart, taking in all saints, and all men, and all needs. An attempt has been made in these helps to indicate what the chief subjects are that need prayer, and that ought to interest every Christian.

It will be felt difficult by many to pray for such large spheres as are sometimes mentioned. Let it be understood that in each case we may make special intercession for our own circle of interest coming under that heading. And it is hardly needful to say, further, that where one subject appears of more special interest or urgency than another we are free for a time, day after day, to take up that subject. If only time be really given to intercession, and the spirit of believing intercession be cultivated, the object is attained. While, on the one hand, the heart must be enlarged at times to take in all, the more pointed and definite our prayer can be, the better. With this view paper is left blank on which we can write down special petitions we desire to urge before God.

3. *Answers to Prayer.* — More than one little book has been published in which Christians may keep a register of their petitions, and note when they are answered. Room has been left on every page for this, so that more definite petitions with regard to individual souls or special spheres of work may be recorded, and the answer expected. When we pray for all saints, or for missions in general, it is difficult to know when or how our prayer is answered, or whether our prayer has had any part in bringing the answer. It is of extreme importance that we should prove that God hears us, and to this end take note of what answers to look for, and when they come. On the day of praying for all saints, take the saints of your congregation, or in your prayer meeting, and ask for a revival among them. Take, in connection with missions, some special station or missionary you are interested in, or more than one, and plead for blessing. And expect and look for its coming, that you may praise God.

4. *Prayer Circles.* — In publishing this invitation to intercession, there is no desire to add another to the many existing prayer unions or praying bands. The first object is to stir the many Christians who practically, through ignorance of their calling or unbelief as to their prayer availing much, take but very little part in the work of intercession; and then to help those who do pray to some fuller apprehension of the greatness of the work, and the need of giving their whole strength to it. There is a circle of prayer which asks for prayer on the first day of every month for the fuller manifestation of the power of the Holy Spirit throughout the Church. I have given the words of that invitation as subject for the first day, and taken the same thought as keynote throughout. The more one thinks of the need and the promise, and the greatness of the obstacles to be overcome in prayer, the more one feels it must become our lifework day by day, that to which every other interest is subordinated.

But while not forming a large prayer union, it is suggested that it may be found helpful to have small prayer circles to unite in prayer, either for one month, with some special object introduced daily along with the others, or through a year or longer, with the view of strengthening each other in the grace of intercession. If a minister were to invite some of his neighboring brethren to join for some special requests along with the printed subjects for supplication, or a number of the more earnest members of his congregation to unite in prayer for revival, some might be trained to take their place in the great work of intercession, who now stand idle because no man hath hired them.

5. *Who is Sufficient for These Things?* — The more we study and try to practice this grace of intercession, the more we become overwhelmed by its greatness and our feebleness. Let every such impression lead us to listen: *My grace is sufficient for thee,* and to answer truthfully: *Our sufficiency is of God.* Take courage; it is in the intercession of Christ you are called to take part. The burden and the agony, the triumph and the victory are all His. Learn from Him, yield to His Spirit in you, to know how to pray. He gave Himself a sacrifice to God for men, that He might have the right and power of intercession. "He bare the sin of many, and made intercession for the transgressors." Let your faith rest boldly on His finished work. Let your heart wholly identify itself with Him in His death and His life. Like Him, give yourself to God a sacrifice for men; it is your highest nobility; it is your true and full union with Him; it will be to you, as to Him, your power of intercession. Beloved Christian! come and give your whole heart and life to intercession, and you will know its blessedness and its power. God asks nothing less; the world needs nothing less; Christ asks nothing less; let us offer to God nothing less.

FIRST DAY

What to Pray — *For the Power of the Holy Spirit*

I bow my knees unto the Father, that He would grant you that ye may be strengthened with power through His Spirit. — Eph. 3:14-16.

Wait for the promise of the Father. —Acts 1:4.

"The fuller manifestation of the grace and energy of the blessed Spirit of God, in the removal of all that is contrary to God's revealed will, so that we grieve not the Holy Spirit, but that He may work in mightier power in the Church, for the exaltation of Christ and the blessing of souls."

God has one promise to and through His exalted Son; our Lord has one gift to His Church; the Church has one need; all prayer unites in the one petition — the power of the Holy Spirit. Make it your one prayer.

How to Pray — *As a Child Asks a Father*

If a son ask bread of any of you that is a father, will he give him a stone? How much more shall your Heavenly Father give the Holy Spirit to them that ask Him? —Luke 11:11,13.

Ask as simply and trustfully as a child asks bread. You can do this because *"God hath sent forth the Spirit of his Son into your hearts crying, Abba, Father."* This Spirit is in you to give you childlike confidence. In the faith of His praying in you, ask for the power of that Holy Spirit everywhere. Mention places or circles where you specially ask it to be seen.

Special Petitions

SECOND DAY

What to Pray — *For the Spirit of Supplication*

The Spirit Himself maketh intercession for us. —Rom. 8:26.

I will pour out the Spirit of Supplication. —Zech. 12:10.

"The evangelization of the world depends first of all upon a revival of prayer. Deeper than the need of men — aye, deep down at the bottom of our spiritless life — is the need for the forgotten secret of prevailing, world-wide prayer."

Every child of God has the Holy Spirit in him to pray. God waits to give the Spirit in full measure. Ask for yourself, and all who join, the outpouring of the Spirit of Supplication. Ask it for your own prayer circle.

How to Pray — *In the Spirit*

With all prayer and supplication, praying at all seasons in the Spirit. —Eph. 6:18.

Praying in the Holy Spirit. —Jude 20.

Our Lord gave His disciples on His resurrection day the Holy Spirit to enable them to wait for the full outpouring on the day of Pentecost. It is only in the power of the Spirit already in us, acknowledged and yielded to, that we can pray for His fuller manifestation. Say to the Father, it is the Spirit of His Son in you urging you to plead His promise.

Special Petitions

THIRD DAY

What to Pray – *For All Saints*

With all prayer and supplication praying at all seasons, and watching thereunto in all perseverance and supplication for all saints. –Eph. 6:18.

Every member of a body is interested in the welfare of the whole, and exists to help and complete the others. Believers are one body, and ought to pray, not so much for the welfare of their own church or society, but, first of all, for all saints. This large, unselfish love is the proof that Christ's Spirit and Love are teaching them to pray. Pray first for all and then for the believers around you.

How to Pray – *In the Love of the Spirit*

By this shall all men know that ye are My disciples, if ye have love one to another. –John 13:35.

I pray that they all may be one, that the world may believe that Thou didst send Me. –John 17:21.

I beseech you, brethren, by the love of the Spirit, that ye strive together with me in your prayers to God for me. –Rom. 15:30.

Above all things being fervent in your love among yourselves. –1 Pet. 4:8.

If we are to pray we must love. Let us say to God we do love all His saints; let us say we love specially every child of His we know. Let us pray with fervent love, in the love of the Spirit.

Special Petitions

FOURTH DAY

What to Pray – *For the Spirit of Holiness*

God is the Holy One. His people is a holy people. He speaks: *I am holy: I am the Lord which make you holy.* Christ prayed: *Sanctify them. Make them holy through Thy Truth.* Paul prayed: *God establish your hearts unblameable in holiness. God sanctify you wholly!*

Pray for all saints – God's holy ones – throughout the Church, that the Spirit of holiness may rule them. Specially for new converts. For the saints in your own neighborhood or congregation. For any you are specially interested in. Think of their special need, weakness, or sin, and pray that God may make them holy.

How to Pray – *Trusting in God's Omnipotence*

The things that are impossible with men are possible with God. When we think of the great things we ask for, of how little likelihood there is of their coming, of our own insignificance, prayer is not only wishing, or asking, but believing and accepting. Be still before God and ask Him to let you know Him as the Almighty One, and leave your petitions with Him who doeth wonders.

Special Petitions

FIFTH DAY

What to Pray — *That God's People May Be Kept from the World*

Holy Father, keep through Thine own name those whom Thou hast given Me. I pray not that Thou shouldest take them out of the world, but that Thou shouldest keep them from the evil. They are not of the world, even as I am not of the world. —John 17:11, 15, 16.

In the last night Christ asked three things of His disciples: that they might be kept as those who are not of the world; that they might be sanctified; that they might be one in love. You cannot do better than pray as Jesus prayed. Ask for God's people that they may be kept separate from the world and its spirit; that they, by the Spirit, may live as those who are not of the world.

How to Pray — *Having Confidence before God*

Beloved, if our heart condemn us not, then have we confidence toward God. And whatsoever we ask, we receive of Him, because we keep His commandments, and do those things that are pleasing in His sight. — 1 John 3:21, 22.

Learn these words by heart. Get them into your heart. Join the ranks of those who, with John, draw near to God with an assured heart, that does not condemn them, having confidence toward God. In this spirit pray for your brother who sins (1 John 5: 16). In the quiet confidence of an obedient child, plead for those of your brethren who may be giving way to sin. Pray for all to be kept from the evil. And say often, "What we ask, we receive, because we keep and do."

Special Petitions

SIXTH DAY

What to Pray – *For the Spirit of Love in the Church*

I pray that they may be one, even as we are one: I in them and Thou in Me; that the world may know that Thou hast sent Me, and hast loved them, as Thou hast loved Me . . . that the love wherewith Thou hast loved Me may be in them, and I in them. —John 17:22, 23, 26.
The fruit of the Spirit is love. —Gal. 5:22.

Believers are one in Christ, as He is one with the Father. The love of God rests on them, and can dwell in them. Pray that the power of the Holy Ghost may so work this love in believers, that the world may see and know God's love in them. Pray much for this.

How to Pray – *As One of God's Remembrancers*

I have set watchmen on thy walls, which shall never hold their peace day nor night: ye that are the Lord's remembrancers, keep not silence, and give Him no rest.—Isa. 62:6.

Study these words until your whole soul be filled with the consciousness, I am appointed intercessor. Enter God's presence in that faith. Study the world's need with that thought – it is my work to intercede; the Holy Spirit will teach me for what and how. Let it be an abiding consciousness: My great lifework, like Christ's, is intercession – to pray for believers and those who do not yet know God.

Special Petitions

SEVENTH DAY

What to Pray – *For the Power of the Holy Spirit on Ministers*

I beseech you that ye strive together with me in your prayers to God for me. –Rom. 15:30.

He will deliver us; ye also helping together on our behalf by your supplication. –2 Cor. 1:10, 11.

What a great host of ministers there is in Christ's Church. What need they have of prayer. What a power they might be, if they were all clothed with the power of the Holy Ghost. Pray definitely for this; long for it. Think of your minister, and ask it very specially for him. Connect every thought of the ministry, in your town or neighborhood or the world, with the prayer that all may be filled with the Spirit. Plead for them the promise, *"Tarry until ye be clothed with power from on high."* Luke 24:49. *"Ye shall receive power, when the Holy Ghost is come upon you."* Acts 1:8.

How to Pray – *In Secret*

But thou, when thou prayest, enter into thy inner chamber, and having shut thy door, pray to thy Father which is in secret. –Matt. 6:6.

He withdrew again into the mountain to pray, Himself alone. –Matt. 14:23; John 6:15.

Take time and realize, when you are alone with God: Here am I now, face to face with God, to intercede for His servants. Do not think you have no influence, or that your prayer will not be missed. Your prayer and faith will make a difference. Cry in secret to God for His ministers.

Special Petitions

EIGHTH DAY

What to Pray – *For the Spirit on All Christian Workers*

Ye also helping together on our behalf; that for the gift bestowed upon us by means of many, thanks may be given by many on our behalf. –2 Cor. 1:11.

What multitudes of workers in connection with our churches and missions, our railways and postmen, our soldiers and sailors, our young men and young women, our fallen men and women, our poor and sick! God be praised for this! What could they not accomplish if each were living in the fullness of the Holy Spirit? Pray for them; it makes you a partner in their work, and you will praise God each time you hear of blessing anywhere.

How to Pray – *With Definite Petitions*

What wilt thou that I should do unto thee? – Luke 18:41.

The Lord knew what the man wanted, and yet He asked him. The utterance of our wish gives point to the transaction in which we are engaged with God, and so awakens faith and expectation. Be very definite in your petitions, so as to know what answer you may look for. Just think of the great host of workers, and ask and expect God definitely to bless them in answer to the prayer of His people. Then ask still more definitely for workers around you. Intercession is not the breathing out of pious wishes; its aim is – in believing, persevering prayer – to receive and bring down blessing.

Special Petitions

NINTH DAY

What to Pray – *For God's Spirit on Our Mission Work*

The evangelization of the world depends first of all upon a revival of prayer. Deeper than the need for men – aye, deep down at the bottom of our spiritless life, is the need for the forgotten secret of prevailing, world-wide prayer.

As they ministered to the Lord, and fasted, the Holy Ghost said, Separate Me Barnabas and Saul. Then when they had fasted and prayed, they sent them away. So they, being sent forth by the Holy Ghost, departed. –Acts 13:2, 3, 4.

Pray that our mission work may all be done in this spirit – waiting on God, hearing the voice of the Spirit, sending forth men with fasting and prayer. Pray that in our churches our mission interest and mission work may be in the power of the Holy Spirit and of prayer. It is a Spirit-filled, praying Church that will send out Spirit-filled missionaries, mightily in prayer.

How to Pray – *Take Time*

I give myself unto prayer. –Ps. 109:4.
We will give ourselves continually to prayer. –Acts 6:4.
Be not rash with thy mouth, and let not thine heart be hasty to utter anything before God. –Eccles. 5:2.
And He continued all night in prayer to God. –Luke 6:12.

Time is one of the chief standards of value. The time we give is a proof of the interest we feel.

We need time with God – to realize His presence; to wait for Him to make Himself known; to consider and feel the needs we plead for; to take our place in Christ; to pray till we can believe that we have received. Take time in prayer, and pray down blessing on the mission work of the Church.

Special Petitions

TENTH DAY

What to Pray – *For God's Spirit on Our Missionaries*

What the world needs today is not only more missionaries, but the outpouring of God's Spirit on everyone whom He has sent out to work for Him in the foreign field.

Ye shall receive power, when the Holy Ghost is come upon you: and ye shall be My witnesses unto the uttermost part of the earth. —Acts 1:8.

God always gives His servants power equal to the work He asks of them. Think of the greatness and difficulty of this work, — casting Satan out of his strongholds — and pray that everyone who takes part in it may receive and do all his work in the power of the Holy Ghost. Think of the difficulties of your missionaries, and pray for them.

How to Pray – *Trusting God's Faithfulness*

He is faithful that promised. She counted Him faithful who promised. —Heb. 10:23; 11:11.

Just think of God's promises to His Son, concerning His kingdom; to the Church, concerning the heathen; to His servants, concerning their work; to yourself, concerning your prayer; and pray in the assurance that He is faithful, and only waits for prayer and faith to fulfil them. *"Faithful is He that calleth you"* (to pray), *"who also will do it"* (what He has promised). 1 Thess. 5:24.

Take up individual missionaries, make yourself one with them, and pray till you know that you are heard. Oh, begin to live for Christ's kingdom as the one thing worth living for!

Special Petitions

ELEVENTH DAY

What to Pray – *For More Laborers*

Pray ye therefore the Lord of the harvest, that He send forth labourers into His harvest. – Matt. 9:38.

What a remarkable call of the Lord Jesus for help from His disciples in getting the need supplied. What an honor put upon prayer. What a proof that God wants prayer and will hear it.

Pray for laborers, for all students in theological seminaries, training homes, Bible institutes, that they may not go, unless He fits them and sends them forth; that our churches may train their students to seek for the sending forth of the Holy Spirit; that all believers may hold themselves ready to be sent forth, or to pray for those who can go.

How to Pray – *In Faith, Nothing Doubting*

Jesus saith unto them, Have faith in God. Whosoever shall say unto this mountain, Be thou removed, and be thou cast into the sea; and shall not doubt in his heart, but shall believe that what he saith shall come to pass, he shall have it. –Mark 11:22, 23.

Have faith in God! Ask Him to make Himself known to you as the faithful mighty God, who worketh all in all; and you will be encouraged to believe that He can give suitable and sufficient laborers, however impossible this appears. But, remember, in answer to prayer and faith.

Apply this to every opening where a good worker is needed. The work is God's. He can give the right workman. But He must be asked and waited on.

Special Petitions

TWELFTH DAY

What to Pray – *For the Spirit to Convince the World of Sin*

I will send the Comforter to you. And He, when He is come, will convict the world in respect of sin. —John 16:7, 8.

God's one desire, the one object of Christ's being manifested, is to take away sin. The first work of the Spirit on the world is conviction of sin. Without that, no deep or abiding revival, no powerful conversion. Pray for it, that the gospel may be preached in such power of the Spirit, that men may see that they have rejected and crucified Christ, and cry out, What shall we do?

Pray most earnestly for a mighty power of conviction of sin wherever the gospel is preached.

How to Pray – *Stir Up Yourself to Take Hold of God's Strength*

Let him take hold of My strength, that he may make peace with Me. —Isa. 27:5.

There is none that calleth upon Thy name, that stirreth up himself to take hold of Thee. —Isa. 64:7.

Stir up the gift of God which is in thee. —2 Tim. 1:6.

First, take hold of God's strength. God is a Spirit. I cannot take hold of Him, and hold Him fast, but by the Spirit. Take hold of God's strength, and hold on till it has done for you what He has promised. Pray for the power of the Spirit to convict of sin.

Second, stir up yourself — the power is in you by the Holy Spirit — to take hold. Give your whole heart and will to it, and say, I will not let Thee go except Thou bless me.

Special Petitions

22

THIRTEENTH DAY

What to Pray -- *For the Spirit of Burning*

And it shall come to pass, that he that is left in Zion shall be called holy: when the Lord shall have washed away the filth of the daughters of Zion, by the spirit of judgment and the spirit of burning. —Isa. 4:3, 4.

A washing by fire! a cleansing by judgment! He that has passed through this shall be called holy. The power of blessing for the world, the power of work and intercession that will avail, depends upon the spiritual state of the Church; and that can only rise higher as sin is discovered and put away. Judgment must begin at the house of God. There must be conviction of sin for sanctification. Beseech God to give His Spirit as a spirit of judgment and a spirit of burning — to discover and burn out sin in His people.

How to Pray -- *In the Name of Christ*

Whatsoever ye shall ask in My name, that will I do. If ye shall ask Me anything in My name, that will I do. —John 14:13, 14.

Ask in the name of your Redeemer God, who sits upon the throne. Ask what He has promised, what He gave His blood for, that sin may be put away from among His people. Ask — the prayer is after His own heart — for the spirit of deep conviction of sin to come among His people. Ask for the spirit of burning. Ask in the faith of His name — the faith of what He wills, of what He can do — and look for the answer. Pray that the Church may be blessed, to be made a blessing in the world.

Special Petitions

FOURTEENTH DAY

What to Pray – *For the Church of the Future*

That the children might not be as their fathers, a generation that set not their heart aright, and whose spirit was not steadfast with God. —Ps. 78:8.

I will pour My Spirit upon thy seed, and My blessing upon thy offspring. —Isa. 44:3.

Pray for the rising generation, who are to come after us. Think of the young men and women and children of this age, and pray for all the agencies at work among them; that in associations and societies and unions, in homes and schools, Christ may be honored, and the Holy Spirit get possession of them. Pray for the young of your neighborhood.

How to Pray – *With the Whole Heart*

The Lord grant thee according to thine own heart. —Ps. 20:4.

Thou hast given him his heart's desire. —Ps. 21:2.

I cried with my whole heart; hear me, O Lord. —Ps. 119:145.

God lives, and listens to every petition with His whole heart. Each time we pray the whole Infinite God is there to hear. He asks that in each prayer the whole man shall be there too; that we shall cry with our whole heart. Christ gave Himself to God for men; and so He takes up every need into His intercession. If once we seek God with our whole heart, the whole heart will be in every prayer with which we come to this God. Pray with your whole heart for the young.

Special Petitions

FIFTEENTH DAY

What to Pray – *For Schools and Colleges*

As for Me, this is My covenant with them, saith the Lord: My Spirit that is upon thee, and My words which I have put in thy mouth, shall not depart out of thy mouth, nor out of the mouth of thy seed, nor out of the mouth of thy seed's seed, saith the Lord, from henceforth and for ever. —Isa. 59:21.

The future of the Church and the world depends, to an extent we little conceive, on the education of the day. The Church may be seeking to evangelize the heathen, and be giving up her own children to secular and materialistic influences. Pray for schools and colleges, and that the Church may realize and fulfill its momentous duty of caring for its children. Pray for godly teachers.

How to Pray – *Not Limiting God*

They limited the Holy One of Israel. —Ps. 78:41.
He did not many mighty works there because of their unbelief. —Matt. 13:58.
Is anything too hard for the Lord? —Gen. 18:14.
Ah, Lord God! Thou hast made the heaven and the earth by Thy great power; there is nothing too hard for Thee. Behold, I am the Lord: is there anything too hard for Me? —Jer. 32:17, 27.

Beware, in your prayer, above everything, of limiting God, not only by unbelief, but by fancying that you know what He can do. Expect unexpected things, above all that we ask or think. Each time you intercede, be quiet first and worship God in His glory. Think of what He can do, of how He delights to hear Christ, of your place in Christ, and expect great things.

Special Petitions

SIXTEENTH DAY

What to Pray – *For the Power of the Holy Spirit in Our Sunday Schools*

Thus saith the Lord, Even the captives of the mighty shall be taken away, and the prey of the terrible shall be delivered: for I will contend with him that contendeth with thee, and I will save thy children. —Isa. 49:25.

Every part of the work of God's Church is His work. He must do it. Prayer is the confession that He will — the surrender of ourselves into His hands to let Him — work in us and through us. Pray for the hundreds of thousands of Sunday School teachers, that those who know God may be filled with His Spirit. Pray for your own Sunday School. Pray for the salvation of the children.

How to Pray – *Boldly*

We have a great High Priest, Jesus the Son of God. Let us therefore come boldly unto the throne of grace. —Heb. 4:14, 16.

These hints to help us in our work of intercession — what are they doing for us? Making us conscious of our feebleness in prayer? Thank God for this. It is the very first lesson we need on the way to pray the effectual prayer that availeth much. Let us persevere, taking each subject boldly to the throne of grace. As we pray we shall learn to pray and to believe and to expect with increasing boldness. Hold fast your assurance: it is at God's command you come as an intercessor. Christ will give you grace to pray aright.

Special Petitions

SEVENTEENTH DAY

What to Pray – *For Kings and Rulers*

I exhort therefore, first of all, that supplications, prayers, intercessions, thanksgiving, be made for all men; for kings and all that are in high places; that we may lead a tranquil and quiet life in all godliness and gravity. – 1 Tim. 2:1, 2.

What a faith in the power of prayer! A few feeble and despised Christians are to influence the mighty Roman emperors, and help in securing peace and quietness. Let us believe that prayer is a power that is taken up by God in His rule of the world. Let us pray for our country and its rulers; for all the rulers of the world; for rulers in cities or districts in which we are interested. When God's people unite in this, they may count upon their prayers effecting in the unseen world more than they know. Let faith hold this fast.

How to Pray – *The Prayer before God as Incense*

And another angel came and stood at the altar, having a golden censer; and there was given unto him much incense, that he should add it unto the prayers of all the saints upon the golden altar which was before the throne. And the smoke of the incense, with the prayers of the saints, went up before God out of the angel's hand. And the angel taketh the censer; and he filled it with the fire upon the altar, and cast it upo the earth: and there followed thunder, and voices, and lightning, and an earthquake. –Rev. 8:3-5.

The same censer brings the prayer of the saints before God and casts fire upon the earth. The prayers that go up to heaven have their share in the history of this earth. Be sure that thy prayers enter God's presence.

Special Petitions

EIGHTEENTH DAY

What to Pray — *For Peace*

I exhort therefore, first of all, that supplications be made for kings and all that are in high places; that we may lead a tranquil and quiet life in all godliness and gravity. For this is good and acceptable in the sight of God our Saviour. —1 Tim. 2:1-3.

He maketh wars to cease unto the end of the earth. —Ps. 46:9

What a terrible sight! — the military armaments in which the nations find their pride. What a terrible thought! — the evil passions that may at any moment bring on war. And what a prospect for suffering and desolation that must come. God can, in answer to the prayer of His people, give peace. Let us pray for it, and for the rule of righteousness on which alone it can be stablished.

How to Pray — *With the Understanding*

What is it then? I will pray with the spirit, and I will pray with the understanding. —1 Cor. 14:15.

We need to pray with the spirit, as the vehicle of the intercession of God's Spirit, if we are to take hold of God in faith and power. We need to pray with the understanding, if we are really to enter deeply into the needs we bring before Him. Take time to apprehend intelligently, in each subject, the nature, the extent, the urgency of the request, the ground and way and certainty of God's promise as revealed in His Word. Let the mind affect the heart. Pray with the understanding and with the spirit.

Special Petitions

NINETEENTH DAY

What to Pray – *For the Holy Spirit on Christendom*

Having a form of godliness, but denying the power thereof. —2 Tim. 3:5.

Thou hast a name that thou livest, and thou art dead. —Rev. 3:1.

There are five hundred million nominal Christians. The state of the majority is unspeakably awful. Formality, worldliness, ungodliness, rejection of Christ's service, ignorance, and indifference – to what an extent does all this prevail. We pray for the heathen – oh! do let us pray for those bearing Christ's name – many in worse than heathen darkness.

Does not one feel as if one ought to begin to give up his life, and to cry day and night to God for souls? In answer to prayer God gives the power of the Holy Ghost.

How to Pray – *In Deep Stillness of Soul*

My soul is silent unto God: from Him cometh my salvation. —Ps. 62:1.

Prayer has its power in God alone. The nearer a man comes to God Himself, the deeper he enters into God's will; the more he takes hold of God, the more power in prayer.

God must reveal Himself. If it please Him to make Himself known, He can make the heart conscious of His presence. Our posture must be that of holy reverence, of quiet waiting and adoration.

As your month of intercession passes on, and you feel the greatness of your work, be still before God. Thus you will get power to pray.

Special Petitions

TWENTIETH DAY

What to Pray – *For God's Spirit on the Heathen*

Behold, these shall come from far; and these from the land of Sinim. —Isa. 49:12.

Princes shall come out of Egypt; Ethiopia shall haste to stretch out her hands to God. —Ps. 68:31.

I the Lord will hasten it in his time. —Isa. 60:22.

Pray for the heathen, who are yet without the Word. Think of China, with her three hundred millions — a million a month dying without Christ. Think of Dark Africa, with its two hundred millions. Think of thirty millions a year going down into the thick darkness. If Christ gave His life for them, will you not do so? You can give yourself up to intercede for them. Just begin, if you have never yet begun, with this simple monthly school of intercession. The ten minutes you give will make you feel this is not enough. God's Spirit will draw you on. Persevere, however feeble you are. Ask God to give you some country or tribe to pray for. Can anything be nobler than to do as Christ did? Give your life for the heathen.

How to Pray – *With Confident Expectation of an Answer*

Call unto me, and I will answer thee, and will shew thee great things and difficult, which thou knowest not. —Jer. 33:3.

Thus saith the Lord God: I will yet be inquired of, that I do it. —Ezek. 36:37.

Both texts refer to promises definitely made, but their fulfillment would depend upon prayer: God would be inquired of to do it.

Pray for God's fulfillment of His promises to His Son and His Church, and expect the answer. Plead for the heathen: plead God's promises.

Special Petitions

TWENTY-FIRST DAY

What to Pray – *For God's Spirit on the Jews*

I will pour out upon the house of David, and the inhabitants of Jerusalem, the Spirit of grace and supplications; and they shall look unto Me whom they pierced. —Zech. 12:10.

Brethren, my heart's desire and my supplication to God is for them, that they may be saved. —Rom. 10:1.

Pray for the Jews. Their return to the God of their fathers stands connected, in a way we cannot tell, with wonderful blessing to the Church, and with the coming of our Lord Jesus. Let us not think that God has foreordained all this, and that we cannot hasten it. In a divine and mysterious way God has connected his filfillment of His promise with our prayer. His Spirit's intercession in us is God's forerunner of blessing. Pray for Israel and the work done among them. And pray too: Amen. Even so, come Lord Jesus!

How to Pray – *With the Intercession of the Holy Spirit*

We know not how to pray as we ought; but the Spirit Himself maketh intercession for us with groanings which cannot be uttered. —Rom. 8:26

In your ignorance and feebleness believe in the secret indwelling and intercession of the Holy Spirit within you. Yield yourself to His life and leading habitually. He will help your infirmities in prayer. Plead the promises of God even where you do not see how they are to be fulfilled. God knows the mind of the Spirit, because He maketh intercession for the saints according to the will of God. Pray with the simplicity of a little child; pray with the holy awe and reverence of one in whom God's Spirit dwells and prays.

Special Petitions

TWENTY-SECOND DAY

What to Pray — *For All Who Are in Suffering*

Remembering them that are in bonds, as bound with them; them that are evil entreated, as being yourselves in the body. —Heb. 13:3.

What a world of suffering we live in! How Jesus sacrificed all and identified Himself with it! Let us in our measure do so too. The persecuted, the Jews, the famine-stricken millions of India, the hidden slavery of Africa, the poverty and wretchedness of our great cities — and so much more: what suffering among those who know God and who know Him not. And then in smaller circles, in ten thousand homes and hearts, what sorrow. In our own neighborhood, how many needing help or comfort. Let us have a heart for, let us think of the suffering. It will stir us to pray, to work, to hope, to love more. And in a way and time we know not God will hear our prayer.

How to Pray — *Praying always and not fainting*

He spake unto them a parable to the end that they ought always to pray, and not to faint. —Luke 18:1.

Do you not begin to feel prayer is really the help for this sinful world? What a need there is of unceasing prayer! The very greatness of the task makes us despair! What can our ten minutes intercession avail? It is right we feel this: this is the way in which God is calling and preparing us to give our life to prayer. Give yourself wholly to God for men, and amid all your work, your heart will be drawn out to men in love, and drawn up to God in dependence and expectation. To a heart thus led by the Holy Spirit, it is possible to pray always and not to faint.

Special Petitions

Helps to Intercession

TWENTY-THIRD DAY

What to Pray – *For the Holy Spirit in Your Own Work*

I labour, striving according to His working, which worketh in me mightily. —Col. 1:29.

You have your own special work; make it a work of intercession. Paul labored, striving according to the working of God in him. Remember, God is not only the Creator, but the Great Workman, who worketh all in all. You can only do your work in His strength, by His working in you through the Spirit. Intercede much for those among whom you work, till God gives you life for them.

Let us all intercede too for each other, for every worker throughout God's Church, however solitary or unknown.

How to Pray – *In God's Very Presence*

Draw nigh to God, and He will draw nigh to you. — Jas. 4:8.

The nearness of God gives rest and power in prayer. The nearness of God is given to him who makes it his first object. "Draw nigh to God"; seek the nearness to Him, and He will give it; "He will draw nigh to you." Then it becomes easy to pray in faith.

Remember that when first God takes you into the school of intercession it is almost more for your own sake than that of others. You have to be trained to love, and wait, and pray, and believe. Only persevere. Learn to set yourself in His presence, to wait quietly for the assurance that He draws nigh. Enter His holy presence, tarry there, and spread your work before Him. Intercede for the souls you are working among. Get a blessing from God, His Spirit into your own heart, for them.

Special Petitions

TWENTY-FOURTH DAY

What to Pray – *For the Spirit on Your Own Congregation*

Beginning at Jerusalem. —Luke 24:47.

Each one of us is connected with some congregation or circle of believers, who are to us the part of Christ's body with which we come into most direct contact. They have a special claim on our intercession. Let it be a settled matter between God and you that you are to labor in prayer on its behalf. Pray for the minister and all leaders or workers in it. Pray for the believers according to their needs. Pray for conversions. Pray for the power of the Spirit to manifest itself. Band yourself with others to join in secret in definite petitions. Let intercession be a definite work, carried on as systematically as preaching or Sunday School. And pray, expecting an answer.

How to Pray – *Continually*

Watchmen, that shall never hold their peace day or night. —Isa. 62:6.

His own elect, that cry to Him day and night. —Luke 18:7

Night and day praying exceedingly, that we may perfect that which is lacking in your faith. —1 Thess. 3:10.

A widow indeed, hath her hope set in God, and continueth in supplications night and day. —1 Tim. 5:5.

When the glory of God, and the love of Christ, and the need of souls are revealed to us, the fire of this unceasing intercession will begin to burn in us for those who are near and those who are far off.

Special Petitions

TWENTY-FIFTH DAY

What to Pray – *For More Conversions*

He is able to save completely, seeing He ever liveth to make intercession. —Heb. 7:25.

We will give ourselves continually to prayer and the ministry of the word . . . And the word of God increased; and the number of the disciples multiplied exceedingly. —Acts 6:4, 7.

Christ's power to save, and save completely, depends on His unceasing intercession. The apostles' withdrawing themselves from other work to give themselves continually to prayer was followed by the number of the disciples multiplying exceedingly. As we, in our day, give ourselves to intercession, we shall have more and mightier conversions. Let us plead for this. Christ is exalted to give repentance. The Church exists with the Divine purpose and promise of having conversions. Let us not be ashamed to confess our sins and feebleness, and cry to God for more conversions in Christian and heathen lands, of those too whom you know and love. Plead for the salvation of sinners.

How to Pray – *In Deep Humility*

Truth, Lord: yet the dogs eat of the crumbs . . . O woman, great is thy faith: be it unto thee even as thou wilt. —Matt. 15:27, 28.

You feel unworthy and unable to pray aright. To accept this heartily, and to be content still to come and be blest in your unworthiness, is true humility. It proves its integrity by not seeking for anything, but simply trusting His grace. And so it is the very strength of a great faith, and gets a full answer. "Yet the dogs" — let that be your plea as you persevere for someone possibly possessed of the devil. Let not your littleness hinder you for a moment.

Special Petitions

TWENTY-SIXTH DAY

What to Pray — *For the Holy Spirit on Young Converts*

Peter and John prayed for them, that they might receive the Holy Ghost; for as yet He was fallen upon none of them: only they had been baptized into the name of the Lord Jesus. — Acts 8:15, 16.

Now He which establisheth us with you in Christ, and anointed us, is God; who also gave us the earnest of the Spirit in our hearts. —2 Cor. 1:21,22.

How many new converts who remain feeble; how many who fall into sin; how many who backslide entirely. If we pray for the Church, its growth in holiness and devotion to God's service, pray especially for the young converts. How many stand alone, surrounded by temptation; how many have no teaching on the Spirit in them, and the power of God to establish them; how many in heathen lands, surrounded by Satan's power. If you pray for the power of the Spirit in the Church, pray especially that every young convert may know that he may claim and receive the fullness of the Spirit.

How to Pray — *Without Ceasing*

As for me, God forbid that I should sin against the Lord in ceasing to pray for you. —1 Sam. 12:23.

It is sin against the Lord to escape praying for others. When once we begin to see how absolutely indispensable intercession is, just as much a duty as loving God or believing in Christ, and how we are called and bound to it as believers, we shall feel that to cease intercession is grievous sin. Let us ask for grace to take up our place as priests with joy, and give our lives to bring down the blessing of heaven.

Special Petitions

TWENTY-SEVENTH DAY

What to Pray – *That God's People May Realize Their Calling*

I will bless thee; and be thou a blessing: IN THEE shall ALL THE FAMILIES OF THE EARTH be blessed. —Gen. 12:2, 3.

God be merciful UNTO US, and bless US, and cause His face to shine UPON US. That Thy way may be known UPON EARTH, Thy saving health AMONG ALL NATIONS. —Ps. 67:1, 2

Abraham was only blessed that he might be a blessing to all the earth. Israel prays for blessing, that God may be known among all nations. Every believer, just as much as Abraham, is only blessed that he may carry God's blessing to the world.

Cry to God that His people may know this, that every believer is only to live for the interests of God and His kingdom. If this truth were preached and believed and practiced, what a revolution it would bring in our mission work. What a host of willing intercessors we should have. Plead with God to work it by the Holy Spirit.

How to Pray – *As One Who Has Accepted for Himself What He Asks for Others*

Peter said, What I have, I give unto thee . . . The Holy Ghost fell on them, as on us at the beginning . . . God gave them the like gift, as He gave unto us. —Acts 3:6; 9:15, 17.

As you pray for this great blessing on God's people, the Holy Spirit taking entire possession of them for God's service, yield yourself to God, and claim the gift anew in faith. Let each thought of feebleness or shortcoming only make you the more urgent in prayer for others; as the blessing comes to them, you too will be helped. With every prayer for conversions or mission work, pray that God's people may know wholly they belong to Him.

Special Petitions

TWENTY-EIGHTH DAY

What to Pray — *That all God's People May Know the Holy Spirit*

The Spirit of truth, whom the world knoweth not; but ye know Him; for He abideth with you, and shall be in you. —John 14:17.

Know ye not that your body is the temple of the Holy Ghost? —1 Cor. 6:19.

The Holy Spirit is the power of God for the salvation of men. He only works as He dwells in the Church. He is given to enable believers to live wholly as God would have them live, in the full experience and witness of Him who saves completely. Pray God that everyone of His people may know the Holy Spirit! That He, in all His fullness, is given to them! That they cannot expect to live as their Father would have, without having Him in His fullness, without being filled with Him! Pray that all God's people, even away in churches gathered out of heathendom, may learn to say: I believe in the Holy Ghost.

How to Pray — *Laboring Fervently in Prayer*

Epaphras, who is one of you, saluteth you, always labouring fervently for you in prayers, that ye may stand perfect and complete in all the will of God. —Col. 4:12.

To a healthy man labor is a delight; in what interests him he labors fervently. The believer who is in full health, whose heart is filled with God's Spirit, labors fervently in prayer. For what? That his brethren may stand perfect and complete in all the will of God; that they may know what God wills for them how He calls them to live, and be led and walk by the Holy Ghost. Labor fervently in prayer that all God's children may know this, as possible, as divinely sure.

Special Petitions

TWENTY-NINTH DAY

What to Pray – *For the Spirit of Intercession*

I chose you, and appointed you, that ye should go and bear fruit; that whatsoever ye shall ask of the Father in My name, He may give it to you. –John 15:16.

Hitherto have ye asked nothing in My name. In that day ye shall ask in My name. –John 16:24, 26.

Has not our school of intercession taught us how little we have prayed in the name of Jesus? He promised His disciples: In that day, when the Holy Spirit comes upon you, ye shall ask in My name. Are there not tens of thousands with us mourning the lack of the power of intercession? Let our intercession today be for them and all God's children, that Christ may teach us that the Holy Spirit is in us; and what it is to live in His fullness, and to yield ourselves to His intercessional work within us. The Church and the world need nothing so much as a mighty Spirit of Intercession to bring down the power of God on earth. Pray for the descent from heaven of the Spirit of Intercession for a great prayer revival.

How to Pray – *Abiding in Christ*

If ye abide in Me, and My words abide in you, ask whatsoever ye will, and it shall be done to you. –John 15:7.

Our acceptance with God, our access to Him, is all in Christ. As we consciously abide in Him we have the liberty, not a liberty to our old nature or self-will, but the Divine liberty from all self-will, to ask what we will, in the power of the new nature, and it shall be done. Let us keep this place, and believe even now that our intercession is heard, and that the Spirit of Supplication will be given all around us.

Special Petitions

THIRTIETH DAY

What to Pray – *For the Holy Spirit with the Word of God*

Our gospel came not unto you in word only, but also in power, and in the Holy Ghost, and in much assurance. —1 Thess. 1:5.

Those who preached unto you the gospel with the Holy Ghost sent forth from heaven. —1 Pet. 1:12.

What numbers of Bibles are being circulated. What numbers of sermons on the Bible are being preached. What numbers of Bibles are being read in home and school. How little blessing when it comes "in word" only; what Divine blessing and power when it comes "in the Holy Ghost," when it is preached "with the Holy Ghost sent forth from heaven." Pray for Bible circulation, and preaching and teaching and reading, that it may all be in the Holy Ghost, with much prayer. Pray for the power of the Spirit with the word in your own neighborhood, wherever it is being read or heard. Let every mention of "The Word of God" waken intercession.

How to Pray – *Watching and Praying*

Continue steadfastly in prayer, watching therein with thanksgiving; withal praying for us also, that God may open unto us a door for the word. —Col. 4:2, 3.

Do you not see how all depends upon God and prayer? As long as He lives and loves, and hears and works, as long as there are souls with hearts closed to the word, as long as there is work to be done in carrying the word — *Pray without ceasing. Continue steadfastly in prayer, watching therein with thanksgiving.* These words are for every Christian.

Special Petitions

THIRTY-FIRST DAY

What to Pray — *For the Spirit of Christ in His people*

I am the Vine, ye are the branches. —John 15:5.
That ye should do as I have done to you. —John 13:15.

As branches we are to be so like the Vine, so entirely identified with it, that all may see that we have the same nature, and life, and spirit. When we pray for the Spirit, let us not only think of a Spirit of power, but the very disposition and temper of Christ Jesus. Ask and expect nothing less: for yourself, and all God's children, cry for it.

How to Pray — *Striving in Prayer*

That ye strive together with me in your prayers to God for me. —Rom. 15:30.
I would ye knew what great conflict I have for you. —Col. 2:1.

All the powers of evil seek to hinder us in prayer. Prayer is a conflict with opposing forces. It needs the whole heart and all our strength. May God give us grace to strive in prayer till we prevail.

Special Petitions

NOTES

NOTES

NOTES

NOTES

NOTES

NOTES

NOTES